At 4:30 a.m. on April 12, 1861, an artillery shell streaked through the pre-dawn darkness above Charleston harbor and exploded in a burst of smoke and flame over Fort Sumter. It was the opening shot of the American Civil War and it ended decades of tension between the North and the South.

The two regions were vastly different. The North was industrial, increasingly urban and progressive; the South was agricultural, rural and traditional. Northerners generally favored a strong national government, while many Southerners were suspicious of Federal power and believed most government should reside with the individual states. Throughout the first half of the 19th century, the two regions had competed to control the nation's government and destiny.

President Lincoln called for 75,000 Northern volunteers.

Returning fire
at Fort Sumter

Leaving for
the War

Northern leaders wanted the Federal government to sponsor railroads, highways and canals and to open the vast Western lands to small farmers. Southern leaders were wary of Federally-assisted development and worried that Northern political power would swell with the admission of Western states. Northerners pushed for high tariffs on imported goods to promote Northern manufacturing; Southerners saw the tariffs as attempts to punish the South for importing manufactured items from abroad at lower cost. The North had almost 90 percent of the nation's manufacturing, most of its railroads and two-thirds of its population. The South grew almost all of the nation's cotton, produced the majority of the nation's military leaders and had provided nine of the country's first 15 presidents. Onto this smoldering fire of sectional rivalry and competition was poured the explosive fuel of slavery.

Waiting for a call to action.

In the South, volunteers rushed to bear arms.

Although other Western nations had discontinued slavery — England had ended it in 1833 — it still existed in America at mid-century. It had begun as a national institution (slavery was legal in New York for almost two centuries and not abolished until 1827), but by 1860 it existed mainly in the South. Even so, less than 20 percent of Southerners were slave owners, and the movement to abolish slavery had originally been most active among Southerners. By 1860, however, harsh political debate, public criticism by Northern abolitionists, and the rise of a cotton-based economy had made many Southerners defensive of slavery and the Southern lifestyle. Northern leaders viewed the South as defiant; Southern leaders saw the North as threatening.

In the North, thousands marched away to war.

1861

General Stonewall
Jackson says
goodbye to wife
Mary Anne

Jefferson Davis

Abraham Lincoln

Confederate
Cavalry

In 1860, Abraham Lincoln became the first Republican President.

When the Republican party — which many Southerners viewed as anti-Southern — came to power in 1860 with the election of Abraham Lincoln, nine Southern states led by South Carolina seceded from the Union, proclaimed Southern independence and formed the Confederate States of America. The smoldering tensions ignited at Fort Sumter. The fort's commander, Major Robert Anderson, had secretly moved his Federal troops from another post to Fort Sumter, which was more easily defended and also dominated Charleston's harbor.

The fort became the center of a crisis standoff between Federal authorities who claimed the fort as U.S. property, and Confederate officials who saw Anderson's refusal to evacuate Fort Sumter as an act of war. Despite pleas and warnings from Confederate leaders, the Lincoln administration finally decided to dispatch a flotilla of warships to resupply the fort's garrison. Alarmed Southern officials, led by Confederate President Jefferson Davis, viewed the challenge as a test of Southern sovereignty. When the Federal warships neared Charleston, Anderson was again asked to surrender. When the major declined, Davis ordered Southern forces under General P.G.T. Beauregard to open fire on Fort Sumter, which soon surrendered without loss of life. In response, President Lincoln called for 75,000 volunteers to invade the South. Two more states — North Carolina and Virginia — then joined the Confederacy, and President Davis called for 100,000 volunteers to defend the South. The years of distrust and debate between North and South had erupted in war; when the fighting ended more than 620,000 Americans would be dead — President Lincoln among them — and much of the South would lie in ruins.

General P.G.T. Beauregard

General J.E.B. Stuart: Lee's Cavalry commander.

Union
Cavalry

Stonewall
Jackson at First
Manassas

Hopes that the war would be quick and bloodless died forever at the Battle of First Manassas, which was the first major land battle of the war. Although both sides struggled awkwardly through the battle, Confederate forces under Generals Joseph E. Johnston and P.G.T. Beauregard defeated an overconfident Northern army under General Irvin McDowell and sent it retreating back to Washington, D.C. in panic. The battle's casualties — almost 5,000 dead, wounded and missing — would pale in comparison to the carnage to come, but First Manassas was the bloodiest battle in American history at the time. It also demonstrated the need for properly trained armies and provided a lasting nickname for General Thomas J. Jackson, an obscure Southern instructor from the Virginia Military Institute, who would afterwards be known as Stonewall Jackson.

The Battle of Wilson's Creek

For the rest of the war's first year, fighting was centered in border states. In Missouri on August 10, 1861, Confederate forces led by General Ben McCullough won a bitter, narrow victory over Northern troops led by General Nathaniel Lyon at the Battle of Wilson's Creek. Strife-torn Missouri remained in the Union. Both sides maneuvered to occupy Kentucky, and Northern forces under General George B. McClellan succeeded in driving Confederate forces from the pro-Union region of western Virginia, which was admitted to the Union two years later as the state of West Virginia. In the meantime, the CSS *Virginia*, a Confederate ironclad warship built on the salvaged hull of the USS *Merrimack*, ravaged the Federal fleet at Hampton Roads, Virginia on March 8, 1862. The next day, the *Virginia* and a newly-built Northern ironclad, the USS *Monitor*, fought to a standoff in the world's first battle between ironclad warships.

The USS Monitor
and the
CSS Virginia

Northern troops
in battle

General George B. McClellan

Fresh from his victories in western Virginia, General McClellan was placed in command of the Federal Army of the Potomac, which he drilled and sharpened, then moved by water to a narrow peninsula between Virginia's James and York Rivers. McClellan was an expert organizer, but a reluctant fighter. His massive army of 105,000 troops lumbered up the peninsula toward the Confederate capital of Richmond in the spring of 1862, and by the end of May was poised on the city's outskirts.

General Robert E. Lee

t the Battle of Seven Pines, McClellan's army withstood a forceful attack led by Confederate General Joseph E. Johnston, but an event near the end of the indecisive battle doomed McClellan's Peninsula Campaign and dramatically shaped the future of the war. Johnston was wounded in the battle and was replaced by another officer: General Robert E. Lee of Virginia. The son of a Revolutionary War hero, Lee was known for his character and intelligence as well as his military ability. He had turned down command of the Northern armies at the beginning of the war and was described by some military leaders as the most capable commander in America.

Lee
and
staff

Lee and Jackson
plan Second
Manassas

Johnny Reb

Reorganizing his forces into the Army of Northern Virginia, Lee promptly launched an offensive known as the Seven Days Campaign and drove McClellan's army back down the Peninsula. The hard-driving Stonewall Jackson, meanwhile, had bewildered and defeated Northern forces in the Shenandoah Valley and had joined Lee's army in time for the Seven Days Battles. Alarmed by the series of Northern defeats, President Lincoln put all Federal armies under the command of General Henry W. Halleck, who ordered McClellan to abandon his Peninsula Campaign and join forces with General John Pope's army in northern Virginia. Before the two Federal armies could unite, however, Lee rapidly moved his army north of Richmond and shattered General Pope's army at the Battle of Second Manassas.

Jackson defeated Federal forces in the Shenandoah Valley.

Antietam was the bloodiest day of the war.

ollowing up on his decisive victory, Lee took his army across the Potomac River into Maryland, heading for Pennsylvania. He wanted to take the war to the North, win a major battle and turn the fall Congressional elections against Lincoln, hoping that would be enough to win Southern independence. The invasion began successfully — Stonewall Jackson captured Harpers Ferry and 10,000 Northern troops — but a lost copy of Lee's marching orders was discovered by Northern troops and taken to General McClellan, whose army had moved north searching for Lee. Although he now knew where to find Lee's army, McClellan inexplicably hesitated, giving Lee time to hurriedly prepare for battle.

Stonewall Jackson captured 10,000 Northern troops at Harpers Ferry.

1862

Northern troops turned back Lee's invasion at Antietam

Antietam allowed
Lincoln to issue the
Emancipation
Proclamation

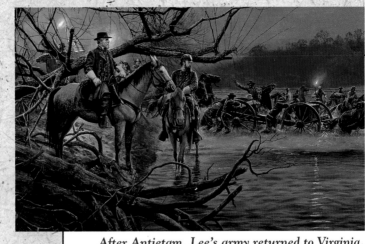

After Antietam, Lee's army returned to Virginia.

he two armies met on September 17, 1862 near Sharpsburg, Maryland and fought the Battle of Antietam. It was the bloodiest single day of the Civil War with more than 26,000 casualties. Although heavily outnumbered, Lee's army withstood McClellan's attack, but the battle ended the 1862 Confederate attempt to invade the North. The Federal army's success at turning back the Confederate invasion gave President Lincoln the opportunity to issue the Emancipation Proclamation, which declared the Confederacy's slaves to be free. Although the Emancipation Proclamation did not free slaves in pro-Union states like Delaware and Missouri, it made ending slavery a Northern war goal, and encouraged the 13th Amendment that would end slavery in 1865.

The 13th Amendment ended slavery.

Lee's strategy at Fredericksburg produced a disastrous Northern defeat.

Jackson, Lee and Stuart plan a surprise attack.

incoln continued to search for a Northern general who could match Lee in Virginia, and replaced General McClellan with General Ambrose E. Burnside as commander of the Army of the Potomac. Lee delivered Burnside a disastrous defeat at the Battle of Fredericksburg on December 13, 1862, and Lincoln then named General Joseph Hooker as Burnside's replacement. In May of 1863, Hooker took his army of 134,000 troops and exercised a brilliant maneuver that threatened Lee's vastly outnumbered army. "I've got Lee just where I want him," Hooker proclaimed. But Lee reacted with a bold gamble. Alerted to a weakness in the Federal line by his cavalry commander, General J.E.B. Stuart, Lee divided his forces and sent Stonewall Jackson and 28,000 troops on a forced march to launch a surprise flank attack that shattered Hooker's army. The Battle of Chancellorsville was Lee's greatest victory, but it came at a severe cost to the South: the irreplaceable Stonewall Jackson was mortally wounded.

Stonewall Jackson was mortally wounded.

Lee and Jackson
at Chancellorsville

1863

Northern Troops
were victorious
at Gettysburg

Lee and his army suffered a staggering defeat.

fter Chancellorsville, Lee again led his army northward toward Pennsylvania, hoping for a great victory on Northern soil that would earn official European recognition of the Confederacy and maybe even win Southern nationhood. It was not to be: Lee reached Pennsylvania this time, but lost the three-day Battle of Gettysburg, July 1-3, 1863, which was the largest battle ever fought in North America.

Lincoln delivered his Gettysburg Address on November 19, 1863.

Although successful on the battle's first day, the Confederates suffered from a series of circumstances and decisions: General J.E.B. Stuart and his cavalry — Lee's "eyes and ears" — were absent on a raid and were unable to provide crucial reconnaissance; Stonewall Jackson's recent death denied Lee the services of his best commander; for various reasons Lee's subordinates were slow to execute his orders; and Lee chose to pursue costly offensive tactics that failed to dislodge General George Meade's Federal forces from their fortified line. Even Pickett's Charge — a valiant mile-long infantry assault by more than 13,000 Confederates — failed to produce the victory Lee sought. Instead of securing Southern nationhood, the war's greatest battle resulted in a staggering Southern defeat and cost Lee 28,000 casualties he could not afford. The Battle of Gettysburg proved to be the turning point of the War Between the States.

Pickett's Charge
at Gettysburg

General
Ulysses S. Grant

Billy Yank

In the Western Theater of the war, meanwhile, Northern forces had recorded a significant string of victories by mid-1863. Northern forces commanded by General Ulysses S. Grant broke the center of the Confederate defensive line in the West in February of 1862 by capturing Forts Henry and Donelson on the Tennessee and Cumberland Rivers. Although cited for bravery in the Mexican War, Grant had experienced repeated failure as an officer and a civilian before the Civil War, and at one point had been reduced to selling firewood on street corners. In the war's first year, however, his fortunes rose as he followed one victory with another. His triumph at Fort Donelson made him famous in the North as "Unconditional Surrender" Grant, and he survived a near disaster in April of 1862, when his army was surprised by a Confederate attack at the bloody Battle of Shiloh.

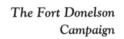

The Fort Donelson Campaign

*General Nathan
Bedford Forrest*

Meanwhile, a Federal naval force under Flag Officer Andrew H. Foote captured Island Number 10, placing the upper Mississippi under Northern control; and the lower Mississippi also fell to the Federals when Captain David G. Farragut's naval operations forced the surrender of New Orleans, the South's largest city, in April of 1862. On July 4, 1863, as Lee's army prepared to retreat southward from Gettysburg, the vital Confederate bastion of Vicksburg on the Mississippi surrendered to General Grant's army after a long, desperate siege. The South was dealt a double disaster: Lee's disastrous defeat at Gettysburg and the loss of Vicksburg, which fully opened the Mississippi to the North and split the Confederacy. Despite fierce raids by General Nathan Bedford Forrest and a dashing raid into Indiana and Ohio by General John Hunt Morgan, the South's fortunes were failing in the Western Theater. General Braxton Bragg invaded Kentucky in the fall of 1862, but failed to recover the state for the South and was turned back by Northern forces at the Battle of Perryville.

Grant at the fall
of Vicksburg

The Battle of Chickamauga

The Battle of Franklin: a Confederate disaster

'The Battle Above the Clouds'
at Lookout Mountain

Withdrawing into Tennessee, Bragg's Army of Tennessee was challenged at year's end by Federal forces under General William S. Rosecrans, who defeated Bragg's army at the Battle of Stone's River near Murfreesboro. Reinforced by troops from Lee's army under General James Longstreet, Bragg won a major Confederate victory, September 19-20, 1863, at the Battle of Chickamauga, but suffered severe defeats at Lookout Mountain and Missionary Ridge and was forced out of Tennessee. General Joseph Johnston was given command of Bragg's army, but was forced by General William T. Sherman to make a stubborn retreat to the defenses of Atlanta. Unable to halt Sherman's advance, Johnston was removed from command by President Davis, who replaced him with General John Bell Hood. After desperate fighting around Atlanta, a vital Southern rail center, Hood gave up the city and marched his outnumbered army through northern Alabama into Tennessee, hoping to lure Sherman and his legions away from Atlanta. Sherman failed to take the bait, and in late 1864 Hood's poorly-led army was ravaged by Federal forces under Generals John M. Schofield and George H. Thomas in devastating battles at Franklin and Nashville.

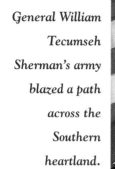

General William Tecumseh Sherman's army blazed a path across the Southern heartland.

Sherman occupied Atlanta and forcibly evacuated the city's residents. He destroyed key military, rail and industrial sites with a blaze that gutted much of Atlanta. Then he led his 62,000 troops on the March to the Sea, cutting a 60-mile-wide swath of destruction across the state with a campaign designed to "make Georgia howl" and bring despair and demoralization to the Southern heartland. In late December of 1864, he was able to offer the port city of Savannah to President Lincoln as a Christmas present. General Grant, meanwhile, had been promoted to general-in-chief of all Northern armies with headquarters in Virginia. Recognizing that the long war had weakened Lee's limited forces, Grant launched a relentless campaign against Lee's army while advancing toward the Confederate capital. Wielding a mighty army of 115,000 against Lee's stubborn 60,000 defenders, Grant forced a series of inconclusive but bloody battles that sapped Lee's strength while moving Northern forces closer to Richmond.

Sherman in
Atlanta

Grant in the
Wilderness

The 54th Massachusetts Infantry

An estimated 25,000 casualties occurred at the Battle of the Wilderness on May 5-6, 1864; the Battle of Spotsylvania, May 8-12, produced 27,000 more; and additional 17,000 were recorded June 1-3 at the Battle of Cold Harbor, where more than 7,000 Northern troops fell in less than a half-hour. Grant had ample replacement troops, but when the campaign ended, Lee and his depleted army were besieged in a thin defensive line stretching from Richmond southward around Petersburg. In grave need of reinforcements, Lee petitioned the Southern government to allow black Southerners to join the Confederate army in exchange for freedom. The Confederate Congress, which had resisted arming slaves, finally agreed to Lee's request and in 1865 the Confederacy began to do what Lincoln eventually had done in the North — train and field black troops.

*Admiral
David Porter*

From Savannah, Sherman moved northward, planning to join forces with Grant. "I almost tremble for her fate," noted Sherman as he unleashed his march-hardened army against secession-leading South Carolina, which suffered mightily. The state capital, Columbia, was set afire, homes and farms were raided and burned, and the state's feeble force of defenders was turned aside as Sherman's army marched unimpeded across the state and into North Carolina. Meanwhile, disaster struck the Confederacy on other fronts. Virginia's fertile and strategic Shenandoah Valley, protected by Confederate successes like the Battle of New Market, was finally devastated by Northern forces under General Philip Sheridan. One by one, Southern seaports were captured or closed by an increasingly powerful Federal navy. In early 1865, a huge Northern amphibious operation under General Alfred H. Terry and Rear Admiral David D. Porter captured Fort Fisher — the South's largest coastal fort — and occupied North Carolina's port city of Wilmington. The South depended on European war material and supplies: closing Wilmington, the South's last major seaport, shut down the lifeline of the Confederacy.

The Battle of
Fort Fisher

☆ ☆ ☆ ☆ ☆ ☆ ☆ ☆ ☆ ☆

Lee surrendered
to Grant at
Appomattox

Lee tried to rally his army at Saylor's Creek.

On April 1, 1865, Grant's troops broke through Lee's weakened line near Petersburg at the Battle of Five Forks, and a day later Grant launched a mammoth assault that dissolved the Confederate line and forced Lee to withdraw. Confederate officials hurriedly evacuated Richmond and on April 3rd Federal troops occupied the Confederate capital. Lee retreated toward Danville, hoping to unite with General Joseph Johnston's army in North Carolina and make a stand, but his beleaguered forces were mauled en route at the Battle of Saylor's Creek. Cut off by Grant's superior forces near Appomattox Court House, Lee realized his army had to "yield to overwhelming numbers and resources." On Palm Sunday, April 9, 1865, Lee surrendered to Grant at Appomattox. The Confederate government quickly dissolved and Southern resistance finally collapsed in a decisive Northern victory.

A victorious President Lincoln pledged to restore the South to the Union "with malice toward none." On April 14, 1865, however, Lincoln was mortally wounded by assassin John Wilkes Booth while attending the theater in Washington. Vice President Andrew Johnson became president, and without Lincoln's leadership a long, harsh era of Reconstruction awaited Southerners. Following Lee's example, Confederate military forces capitulated in a series of surrenders in the weeks following Appomattox. In North Carolina, General Johnston — who had failed to defeat Federal forces at the Battle of Bentonville — surrendered his Confederate army to Sherman on April 26. General Richard Taylor surrendered Confederate forces in Alabama and Mississippi on May 4; General Edmund Kirby Smith surrendered his Trans-Mississippi command on May 26; and on June 23, 1865, General Stand Watie — the last Confederate general to relinquish his command — surrendered his troops in Oklahoma. After four years of bloody conflict, the War Between the States was over.

At war's end,
Southerners and
Northerners
faced the future

Mort Künstler is America's foremost painter of historical subjects. His works have been showcased in ten one-man exhibitions at New York's prestigious Hammer Galleries and at leading museums throughout the country. Künstler has been honored with the first one-man exhibition of original paintings ever shown at the Gettysburg National Military Park and the North Carolina Museum of History in Raleigh. His books include **The American Spirit** with Henry Steele Commager and two best-sellers with text by Pulitzer Prize-winning historian James McPherson: **Gettysburg** and **Images of the Civil War**. The latter book was made into a one-hour special on the Arts and Entertainment Network's **Time Machine**. Künstler's latest book is **Jackson & Lee: Legends in Gray, The Paintings of Mort Künstler,** with text by famed historian James I. Robertson, Jr. Mr. Künstler and his family live in Oyster Bay, New York.

MKünstler

Historian Rod Gragg is the author of **The Civil War Quiz & Fact Book, The Illustrated Confederate Reader, Confederate Goliath: The Battle of Fort Fisher** and other books about the War Between the States.